THE WEAKNESS IN ME

The Weakness in Me
Selected Lyrics

JOAN ARMATRADING

introduced by the author
foreword by GLYN JOHNS

faber

First published in the UK and the USA in 2022
by Faber & Faber Ltd
Bloomsbury House
74–77 Great Russell Street
London WC1B 3DA

Typeset by Hamish Ironside
Printed in the UK by TJ Books Ltd, Padstow, Cornwall

A CIP record for this book
is available from the British Library

ISBN 978–0–571–37759–6

10 9 8 7 6 5 4 3 2 1

Contents

Foreword *by Glyn Johns*

Throughout my career I have had the privilege of working with some exceptional songwriters, and Joan Armatrading is, without doubt, up there with the cream of the crop.

She is totally original, from her extraordinary musicianship to the instantly recognisable sound of her voice performing the huge catalogue of songs she has written. All crafted in her own unique style.

It has always amazed me how a good songwriter is able, in one line of lyric, with a few notes of melody to enhance it, to conjure up any emotion that would take a normal human far greater space and time to express.

As you will see from reading this book, Joan Armatrading is a classic example of this and has created a stunning body of work over the past 50 years that sets her apart from her contemporaries.

Introduction *by Joan Armatrading*

I started writing songs because my mother bought a piano for the front room. As soon as the piano arrived, I started to play it. I can remember lifting the lid as the removers brought the instrument into the room. I just made up things. I had no idea what I was playing, but I knew what sounded good to me, so that's what I went with.

I became fascinated by the guitar because my father had one, but he would hide it. He didn't want me to touch it. I came across my first guitar in a pawn shop. It cost £3. My mother swapped two old prams for it. I still have that guitar.

My father never showed me how to play, but he did show me how to tune it with a funny little melody. I have never seen anyone else tune a guitar like that, but I still use it to this day.

I'm an instinctive writer. I made up my tunes and I made up my lyrics. I never learnt other people's songs; I just made up my own. It's not because I didn't want to learn other people's music, I just found it fascinating to put lyrics and music together, even at the age of fourteen, which is when I started to write songs.

Writing lyrics to songs is very special to me. In very few words over a few minutes you must portray everything the listener needs to hear to capture their imagination. How cool is that!

I write from observation, about how people interact with each other and connect emotionally. The best feeling is having someone say to me that one of my songs helped them to understand their own feelings or how to express themselves to others.

I was born to be a songwriter and it is something that I know, as long as I'm here, I will never stop doing.

I write because I love it!

Conversation

To you it's just another day
And when you see the sun you say
That's the way the day begins
And promises you make
Do you really mean to keep
Or are they words you say
To fill the silent space

And when there's an empty moment
Won't you dedicate it to me
Or is it spent on burning incense
Or painting rooms in white
Lord, won't you call me today
Just to say hello

Conversation is the name of the game
We got phone calls, letters
And brown paper parcels with
To my baby
To my baby
To my baby
With all my love

Back to the Night

Leaves burnt by the sun
And there's no wind blowing
See the motor cars with a smiling face at the wheel
I'm watching the little girls
With their young men at their heels
It's a sunny day
But get me back to the night
'Cause I love that life
Back to the night
Like a skinny burlesque queen
I love a neon
Skyline

Sweet smiling rose
The night life perfume
See the romeos dancing under the moonlight
I said the night
Night was made for romance
You keep your sunny day
Just get me back to the night
'Cause I love that life
Back to the night
Like those skinny burlesque queens
I love a neon skyline
Got the card sharks hustling
At the break of the moon
Gay night walkers
Old blues buskers
All night long there's just so much to do

Just get me back to the night
Oh I love the life
Back to the night
Like a skinny burlesque queen
I love a neon skyline

Cool Blue Stole My Heart

I swear you were not my ambition
A cooling aid was on my mind
I walked up to the bar and I ordered
Then I took my ice outside
I sat down under the hot sun
I looked around at this new land
And then oh
Cool Blue
Long dark
You stole my heart

I woke up first light next morning
And I took a tram to the Leidseplein
I hired a bike and I drove around for hours
I was searching for those dark eyes
I made a stop at the Blue Note
I passed up a chance for some good fun
'Cause of you
Cool Blue
Long dark
Who stole my heart

Get in Touch with Jesus

I wanted to contact Jesus
'Cause of the million and one ways
You said he's good

But if it's too late it's too late
If it's too late for love
I won't take hand-outs
From you
Friends
Just give me wings of doves
Make my mind blank
Set my heart free
Mind that's blank
And a heart that's free
Not a line not a song
To remind me

How come there's kisses at the bottom
When you need
When you need
And no time when your liner
Drifts in
Silver and shining
You broke my heart
Let me tell you I'm hurt
But you know that
I'm too down to cry
I won't cry
I'll turn to Jesus
I'll turn to Jesus
I'll talk to him

And he can help me to help me
Somebody help me
Help me to get in touch with the man
Who can help me dream again

I wanted to contact you now
'Cause of the million and one ways
I know you're good
It's never too late
It's never too late for love

No Love for Free

You come to me trembling, trembling
Shaking at the knees
You say you love me better than
Anyone else can
My head is spinning
I'm flattered
But I don't understand

Every passing hello
How are you
You wanna know his name
Just because I was there when you needed a shoulder
You think I'll take your name
I love for money
I'm flattered
But I can't leave my trade

You will see me holding up some corner store
In my twenties print
And my thumb's turned up
Yes I'm looking for a ride
Jesus woke me up in some
Stranger's bed
They're a lot like you
They want to save my soul

Let me tell you
This lady loves
And she goes where she pleases
No love for free

Down to Zero

Oh the feeling
When you're reeling
You step lightly thinking you're number one
Down to zero
With a word
Leaving
For another one
Now you walk with your feet
Back on the ground
Down to the ground
Down to the ground
Down to the ground
Down to the ground

Brand-new dandy
First-class scene stealer
Walks through the crowd
And takes your man
Sends you rushing to the mirror
Brush your eyebrows and say
There's more beauty in you
Than anyone

Oh remember who walked the warm
Sands beside you
Moored to your heel
Let the waves
Come a-rushing in
She'll take the worry
From your head
But then again

She put
Trouble in your heart instead
Then you'll fall
Down to the ground
Down to the ground

You'll know heartache
Still more crying
When you're thinking of your
Mother's only son
Take to your bed
You say there's peace in sleep
But
You'll dream of love instead
Oh the heartache
You'll find
Can bring more pain
Than a blistering sun
But oh when you fall
Oh when you fall
Fall at my door

Help Yourself

If you're gonna do
Do it right
Don't leave it overnight

If you're gonna help me
Help me now
Another ten minutes
Will be too late

Like a crying child
I need comfort now
Don't pick me up
When the tears are dry
On my face

Need someone
To help me
But not you
You're not ready
Seems you have trouble
Helping yourself

It takes time
To notice
You don't seem to know
Time keeps moving
What you're doing
Is wasting my time
You would help me more
Help me more if you

Helped yourself
Help yourself
Help yourself

You wanna get yourself together
Don't you wanna put yourself to right
I said
Get yourself together
Don't you wanna put yourself to right

I said no
Don't apologise
You've done your best
Seems it still ain't right
Leave me alone
No more to be said
To get it right
You got to do it yourself

I'm going out to help myself
Help myself
Help myself
I'm going out to help myself
Help myself
Help myself

If you're gonna say it
Say it now
Don't leave it overnight

If you're gonna hold me
Hold me tight
I don't wanna leave
Not if it seems alright

Like a crying child
I need comfort now
Don't pick me up
When the tears are dry on my face

You've got to govern
The situation
But not you
You're no
And anyway
Hold up
Hold up
Hold up
You're trying to sort out your mind

You've got to
Get it together
You've got to
Get it together
You would help me more, help me more
If you helped yourself

Love and Affection

I am not in love
But I'm open to persuasion
East or West
Where's the best
For romancing
With a friend
I can smile
But with a lover
I could hold my head back
I could really laugh
Really laugh

Thank you . . .
You took me dancing
Cross the floor
Cheek to cheek
But with a lover
I could really move
Really move
I could really dance
Really dance
Really dance
Really dance
I could really move
Really move
Really move
Really move

Now if I can feel the sun
In my eyes
And the rain on my face

Why can't I
Feel love

I can really love
Really love
Really love
Really love
Really love
Love love love love
Love love love love

Now I got all
The friends that I want
I may need more
But I shall just stick
To those that I have got
With friends I still feel
So insecure

Little darling I believe you could
Help me a lot
Just take my hand
And lead me where you will
No conversation
No wave goodnight
Just make love
With affection

Sing me another love song
But this time
With a little dedication
Sing it sing it
You know that's what I like
Once more with feeling

Give me love
Give me love
Give me love
Love

People

People to the left of me
People to the right
I wanna be along
But it just gets worse all the time
Can't make it work
People all around me
In love
In pain
Some are integrated
Driving me insane
They're gonna drive me right out of my head

Scheming
There's people cheating
Pressure from all sides
Chain you
They try to change you
There's no escaping
People
People
People

Standing right in front of me
Moving up behind
Ringing on my phone
I got no place to hide
Nowhere to go
People all around me
Singing out of tune
Draw me
Don't trace you

Oh . . . leave me alone
I gotta find somewhere else I can go

Once I wanted loving
Somebody of my own
That's all changed
Love somebody of my own
That's all changed
People all around me
In love
In pain
Some are integrated
Driving me insane
They're gonna drive me right out of my head
People
People
People

Save Me

Sinking
Caught up in a whirling motion
Such a strange sensation
The currents uncertain
Like sails of a mill
I spin
Like wheels I move in a circle
While you stand on the bank
Immune or evasive
Throw me a lifeline
Save me

Intimacy and affection
Frozen
In this game of chance
I forfeit
Full hand of love
With no counters
Like a moth
With no flame
To persuade me
Like blood in the rain . . .
Running thin
While you stand on the inside
Looking in
Save me

Inside looking in
Complete in yourself
Throw me a lifeline
Save me

Stand on the bank
Immune or evasive
Throw me a lifeline
Save me

Somebody Who Loves You

I don't know what you're thinking
Should I stay or say goodbye
You blow smoke on the ceiling
You don't wanna look into my eyes
You got somebody who loves you
And I wanna see you fan the fire
Wrap the sheets around you
With me hugged up inside

I wanna see you fan the fire
Come on stoke the blaze
And don't run for cover
You've got someone who loves you
Somebody loves you
You've got someone who loves you
Somebody loves you

Cosy corner your arms around you
So tired of one-night stands
Left with longing from misspent passion
With one more human to despise

You've got somebody who loves you
Don't mine for gold in the dim lit cafes
And as the gypsy once foretold
Love is dark
But no stranger

Mistaken shyness can be costly
Too hasty a goodbye
Then you've lost me
You've got someone who loves you
Somebody loves you

I wanna see you fan the fire
Come on stoke the blaze
And don't run for cover
Mistaken shyness can be costly
Too hasty a goodbye then you've lost me

Tall in the Saddle

Say what you will
You can't take the stars at night
Take your love
But that doesn't stop my life
You've been foolin' around
I looked to you for love
Thought you walked on holy ground
But oh . . .
You're mean

I thought that here
Was a guy
Brave and strong
A brother to his brothers
Brave and strong
Was preaching what to practise
But that don't mean a thing . . .
You're mean

Tall in the saddle
One of these days
You're gonna have to dismount
You don't leave me downhearted
But I'm sorry that you have to go
'Cause we had fun, fun, fun, fun
Fun, fun, fun
We had fun
While it lasted
We had fun
While it lasted

You were God's gift to girls
You persuaded
Then you beat up on their hearts
You made it, you made it
You made it, you made it
Oh . . .
You're mean

Tall in the saddle
One of these days
You're gonna have to dismount
You don't leave me downhearted
But I'm sorry that you have to go
'Cause we had fun, fun, fun, fun
Fun, fun, fun
We had fun
While it lasted
We had fun
While it lasted

You were God's gift to girls
You persuaded
Then you beat up on their hearts
You made it, you made it
You made it, you made it
Oh . . .
You're just mean

Tall in the saddle
One of these days
You're gonna have to dismount
You don't leave me downhearted
But I'm sorry that you have to go
'Cause we had fun, fun, fun, fun
Fun, fun, fun

We had fun
While it lasted
We had fun
While it lasted

Kissin' and a Huggin'

Took my babe walking
We went down to the sea
You know I talked of loving
And you talked of love to me

We sat down under a bus shelter
And talked of other things
But bit by bit by bit by bit
It came round again
How much in love are we

It was a fine thing
We were young
So much love to give
It was the right thing
We were alone
Under the stars

Getting in the mood
Kissing under the
Big
Bright
Shiny stars
That light up the sky
Kissing in front of that old lady
Who just walked past our seat
Getting in the mood
Kissin' and a huggin'
Because

Opportunity

Opportunity
Came to my door
When I was down
On my luck
In the shape
Of an old friend
With a plan
Guaranteed

Showed me the papers
As he walked me to the car
His shoes
Finest leather
He said
You could wear this style
If you follow my advice

He owned a gun
The calibre escaped me
But I noticed
Straight away
It makes me itch
Carried an address
With numbers on the back
And an L-shaped
Bar of iron

What's that for
I asked my man
With eyes
Wide opened

And the knowledge in my head
And he said
Opportunity
Worldwide adventure
Money in the bank

We did the job
The work was so well done
No one saw us coming
Much less leave
But what I dropped
Carried my credentials
And a black and white
Shot of you and me

What's that for
I asked the cop
With eyes of innocence
And the knowledge in my head

And he said
Opportunity
Worldwide adventure
Let me have your hand

Show Some Emotion

Show some emotion
Put expression in your eyes
Light up
If you're feeling happy
But if it's bad
Then let those tears roll down

Some people hurting
Someone choking up inside
Some poor souls dying
Too proud to say
They got no place to lie
And there's people
If they hear a joke
Can keep the laugh
Out of their eye
I said
Show some emotion
Put expression in your eyes
Light up
If you're feeling happy
But if it's bad
Then let those tears roll down

Some people in love
But all they got's a photograph
How can they get it
Too scared
To open their mouth
To ask
I said

Show some emotion
Put expression in your eyes
Light up
If you're feeling happy
But if it's bad
Then let those tears roll down

Come on try
Learn to bleed
When you get a bad fall
Light up
Light up
Light up
If it's nice
But if it's bad
Then let those tears roll down

Willow

I may not be your best
You know good ones
Don't come by the score
If you've got something missing
I'll help you look
You can be sure
And if you want to be alone
Or someone to share a laugh
Whatever you want me to
All you got to do is ask

Thunder
Don't go under the sheets
Lightning
Under a tree
In the rain and snow
I'll be your fireside
Come running to me
When things get out of hand
Running to me
When it's more than you can stand
I said I'm strong
Straight
Willing
To be a
Shelter
In a storm
Your willow oh willow
When the sun is out

A fight with your best girl
Prettiest thing you ever saw
You know I'll listen
Try to get a message to her
And if it's money you want
Or trouble halved
Whatever you want me to
All you got to do is ask
I said I'm strong
Straight
Willing
To be a
Shelter in a storm
Your willow oh willow
When the sun is out

Woncha Come on Home

Every light is on
But all the rooms
Are empty
Except one
Oh babe don't stay too late
You know I hate to be alone
And I'm alone
Babe woncha come on home

There's a madman
Standing on the corner
And he keeps on looking
At my window
Oh babe
Woncha come on home
Home

Every key is turned
And every window's
Bolted from inside
Oh babe
You know I get so scared
You know I couldn't live alone
It's just been confirmed
Babe woncha come on home

Standing on the corner
Is a madman
Looking at my window
Oh babe woncha
Come on home

Home
Babe woncha come on home

There's a man
Standing on the corner
Now a shadow
Moves across the window
Oh babe woncha come on home
Come on home

Baby I

Remember when you took me
Out last night
It was a clear night
The nearest moon I'd ever seen
Filled the sky
Threw light on the city

Remember when you took me
To some party
With your arm around my waist
Planning my weekends
Maybe planning to change
My name
I'm in love
And I got to let you know

Baby I
Want to be
In your loving arms again
Baby I
Want to be
In your loving arms again
Feel you near to me
Babe ah can't you see
So much romance in the air
And all I really want
Is to be with you

I'm trying to get through to you
You see I feel for you
And I won't break free

Our love is natural for me
There's so much romance in the air
And all I really want
Is to be with you

Barefoot and Pregnant

So many ladies love you
With the innocence of a child
A child who believes in God
You keep 'em in luxury
But it's luxury in the dark.

You walk around with a smile
Upon your face
But there's something that
You don't know
Your luck's run out
And it's time for you to know

Everybody told me I was crazy
To try to tame such a wild one
Baby baby baby baby baby
I got myself into this thing
Like I never knew I could and now
I got to get away just as fast as
I can
I got myself into this thing
And I'll find a way out

You gave me babies
To you
That proves your love
Tie my hands with jewels
Barefoot and pregnant you kept me
You sought to
Hide me from the truth
But your lady's done bought

Some shoes
And she's
Steppin' out on the town
Your lady
Took herself in hand
And she's spreading
Herself around

I wanted your love
But not at any price
You're just the hurting kind
Say you want me for yourself
But your
Deeds
Deny it

'Barefoot and Pregnant' is about a man who will give his partner everything,
except he wants her all to himself. He doesn't want her to go out to meet
friends or leave the house. He just wants her to be with him. He gives her
everything, but this is just a way of controlling her.

Flight of the Wild Geese

Sad are the eyes
Yet no tears
The flight of the wild geese
Brings a new hope
Rescue from all this
Old friends
And those newly found
What chance to make it last
When there's danger all around
And reason just ups and disappears
Time is running out
So much to be done
Tell me what more
What more
What more can we do

There were promises made
Plans firmly laid
Now madness prevails
And lies fill the air

What more, oh
What more
What more can we do
What chance to make it last

What more
What more can we do

He Wants Her

He's a tom cat, a stallion
After a lusty mare
She kicks and bucks
With love big eyes
He just hangs on in there

He wants her, and it's simple man
He wants her, 'cause she's his kind
He wants her, he wants her, he wants her

He's a rat, a fighter
They're a match
What he wants he means to get
You better understand

And he wants her, to bear his child
He wants her to love her man
He wants her, he wants her, he wants her

He wants to be a lion to her lamb
You know he means to love her all he can
He wants to be a lion to her lamb
You know he means to love her all he can
He wants her, he wants her, he wants her

He's a fox, a rooster
After a broodin' hen
Watch out ma'am he says you can't
Rough on this male man

He wants her, with all her frills
He wants her, to give him thrills
He wants her, he wants her,
He wants her, he wants her

How Cruel

Some people want to see my blood gush out
And others want to watch while I crawl
I heard somebody say once I was way too black
And someone answered she's not black enough for me
I bite my tongue and it bites me back
I bought a house and the neighbours moved
I had a dog but it was stolen

Some people say that it's comin'
And I'll get it
It must be something I have no control of
They'll put the skin of the fruit on the ground
And I'll slip and fall
Oh how cruel to make a girl cry
Oh how cruel to make a girl cry
Oh how cruel to make a girl cry

I have no hope in hell and I want to get to heaven
Too many lies or not enough sinnin'
Some people say that it's comin'
And I'll get it
It must be something I have no control of
They'll put the skin of the fruit on the ground
And I'll slip and fall
Oh how cruel to make a girl cry
Oh how cruel to make a girl cry

I did have a dog, and it was stolen.

I Really Must Be Going

Told me that you loved me
You've been looking for me all your life
Told you I was married
You said, 'Baby, it don't seem right'

One touch from your fingers and I'm burning
I can't wait to kiss you on the mouth
I can't contain this yearning, and I can't seem to put
    the fire out

I went up to your apartment
Only to be polite
It's late, I started leaving
But you got in the way so nice

That look in your eyes I'm learning
Would melt a tyrant's heart
But I really must be going
And I'll see you later sweetheart

The phone rang in the morning
The day had just begun
I heard your soft voice crying
Told me you were wrong
In time I'd learn to love you
And you had time to spare
And you'd call again tomorrow
And the next day

The midday flight was on time
No time to hesitate
I changed and unchanged my mind
But this one had to stay

I knew that if we started
I'd be lost and so would you
Though we both regret our parting
We are bound to see it through

I still see your face before me
I smell the scent you wore
I hear your soft voice crying
One touch from your fingers and I'm burning
I can't wait to kiss you on the mouth
I can't contain this yearning
And I can't seem to put the fire out

Rosie

He has little red feet
His stocking and his shoes
Lipstick and rouge on his face
He has his hair piled high
Has a red umbrella and carries his head in the sky

And I said
Aw Rosie, don't you do that to the boys
Don't you come on so willin'
Don't you come on so strong
It can be so chillin'
When you act so willin'
And your warmth sets like the sun

He has a little baby brother
A big fat mama
His sister asks for dimes on the street
He doesn't feel insecure
In fact he knows
For sure he can please

I said he's out there right now
Runnin' with the devil
Struttin' down the alleyways
With a nervous young hopeful at his heel
And only satisfaction will drive him away

And I said
Aw Rosie, don't you do that to the boys
Don't you come on so willin'
Don't you come on so strong

It can be so chillin'
When you act so willin'
And your warmth sets like the sun

He's not lookin' for a friend
Not lookin' for a lover
There in the crowded bar
He has rings on his fingers
He's there to tease
Ya know he only wants to take things too far

I wrote 'Rosie' after being shown around New York by a taxi driver who
asked me if I had seen much of the city. When I answered I had not seen
much he offered to show me around. By the way, he did not charge me more
than the fare should have been. In any case he took me to this street where I
saw many transvestites in their high heels, make-up and lovely dresses. This
was in the 1970s, so very progressive perhaps.

All the Way from America

You called all the way from America
And said
Hang on to love
Girl
But the weeks
And the months
And the tears
Passed by
And my eyes couldn't
Stand the strain
Of that promised love
All the way from America

You called all the way from America
And said
I'll soon be home girl
But the years
And the tears
And the fears
Passed by
And my heart couldn't
Stand the pain
Of that promised love
All the way from America
All the way from America

I stayed all along
And I waited 'round
For you to knock at my door
But the knock never came
And no ring at all

And now I sit
And wonder
Why
You made that
First call
All the way from America

I don't believe I'll stay here
I don't think I want to wait here
Anymore
And if you search for me baby
Better bring some more love
Than you declared
All the way from America

I Need You

Late at night
I feel so lonely
Here's a body next to mine
But I'm feeling cold
And baby
In the morning light
When I look in some
Stranger's eyes
It's then I know that
The need in me
Is really
For your paradise

I dance
I sing
But there's something missing
Every night a different name to call
But you know
When I hold 'em tight
I always give the game away
I try so hard
To make it right
But it always ends up the same

You know
I need you
I need you
Like I needed you
The first time we kissed
I need you
And I need you now

And I can't resist
Standing by your door
In case you leave
I miss you mostly in the night
And I miss you
All through the day
I hate myself for hurting you
Yes I know I drove you clean
Away

You know I need you
But now I need you

Me Myself I

I sit here by myself
And you know I love it
You know I don't want someone
To come pay a visit
I wanna be by myself
I came in this world alone
Me myself I

I want to go to China
And to see Japan
I'd like to sail the oceans
Before the seas run dry
I wanna go
By myself
I've just room enough for
One
Me myself I

I wanna be a big shot
And have ninety cars
I wanna have a boyfriend
And a girl
For laughs
But only on Saturday
Six days to be alone
With me myself I
Me myself and I
Just me myself I

Don't want to be the bad guy
Don't want to make a soul cry

It's not that I love myself
I just don't want company
Except
Me
Myself
I

Me myself . . . and I
Just me myself I

I'm Lucky

I'm lucky
I'm lucky
I can walk under ladders
Yes I'm so lucky
That I'm as lucky as me

Struck it rich
Dirty rich
No work
And get richer
And the world
Loves a winner
Yes I'm so happy
That you're happy with me

You are happy too
Ain't you baby

Numero uno
Living for
Right now
And it's
L-I-V-I-N-G
When I'm here with you

I'm lucky
I'm lucky
I don't need a bracelet
No salt
For my shoulder
I don't own a rabbit

No clover
No heather
No cross
No wonder
I'm lucky

The Weakness in Me

I'm not the sort of person
Who falls
In
And quickly
Out
Of love
But to you I gave my affection
Right from the start

I have a lover
Who loves me
How could I break such a heart
Yet still you get my attention

Why do you come here
When you know I've got troubles
Enough
Why do you call me
When you know
I can't answer the phone
Make me lie
When I don't want to
And make someone else
Some kind of an unknowing fool

You make me stay
When I should not
Are you so strong
Or is all the weakness in me
Why do you come here
And pretend

To be just passing by
But I mean to see you
And I mean to hold you
Tightly

Feeling guilty
Worried
Waking from some tormented sleep
This old love has me bound
But the new love cuts deep

If I choose now
I'll lose out
One of you has to fall
And I need you
And you

Drop the Pilot

I'm right on target
My aim is straight
So you're in love
I say
What of it
Things can change
There's always changes
And I wanna try
Some rearranging

Drop the pilot
Try my balloon
Drop the monkey
Smell my perfume
Drop the mahout
I'm the easy rider
Don't use your army
To fight a losing battle

Animal mineral physical spiritual
I'm the one you need
I'm the one you need

You're kissing cousins
There's no smoke
No flame
If you lose that pilot
I can fly your plane
If you want solid ground
Come on and try me

Or I can take you so high
That you're never gonna wanna
Come down

Drop the pilot
Try my balloon
Drop the monkey
Smell my perfume
Drop the mahout
I'm the easy rider
Don't use your army
To fight a losing battle

Animal mineral physical spiritual
I'm the one you need
I'm the one you need
I said
Animal mineral physical spiritual
I'm the one you need
I'm the one you need
I'm the one you need

Eating the Bear

He had me down
But I put up a fight
I saw those teeth
And I groped for my knife
Big brown bear
With the juice from his mouth
He could taste my leg
And he thought he'd got me

But I am eating the bear

He lurked around
'Cause he knew where I lived
I'm in the jungle
And he means to eat me
He means to eat me
He's a hungry bear
He touched my arm
And he thought he'd got me

But I am eating the bear

Some days the bear
Will eat you

Some days you eat the bear

And I am eating the bear

It's not just girls
He eats who he wants
He's big and strong
Fights dirty
And mean
If you spill some blood
He'll smell you for miles
You better watch out
'Cause he's right behind you

But I am eating the bear

Everybody Gotta Know

I've done it myself
I've done things
I never thought I would do
We all make mistakes
And I'm no exception
Sometimes
I think I've told it all
So plainly
But there's no one there
To hear the words I say
Sometimes
It all sounds so crazy
Your version of the story
That I know
Oh when your memory
Fails you

Everybody
Gotta know this feeling
Everybody gotta know
Everybody gotta know this feeling
Inside

I've been there myself
I have been some place
I never would go to
Just not my style
But persuasion made me
Open my mind
Sometimes
I think I know it all so clearly

But then someone comes
And shows another way
Sometimes
I think that I am going crazy
My character changes
For one day
Oh when your habits fail you

Everybody
Gotta know this feeling
Everybody gotta know
Everybody gotta know this feeling
Inside

Frustration

Throw it at the wall
Stamp your feet
Punch out a guy, any guy you meet
Hey Chainsaw, I'm bigger than you
Hey Chainsaw, I'm bigger than you

Frustration, you'll find it there at the bottom of the stairs
Frustration, you'll find it there on the factory floor
Frustration, you'll find it there in the body of a man
Frustration, it's frustrating

Material
It's who you know
It's sexual
It's the way it goes
Hey Chainsaw, I'm bigger than you
Hey Chainsaw, I'm bigger than you

Frustration, it makes you do things
Frustration, it'll change your colour, it'll make you green
Frustration, and if it makes you green it can make you blue

Smoke in the engine
Slide in the pool
The heat's too hot
And the cold's too cool

Frustration, it'll make you feel like you wanna break down
Frustration, the strength to break you to the mind of a child
Frustration, the boogie man put a hex on you
Frustration, bogady bogady whoo

Hey Chainsaw, I'm bigger than you
Hey Chainsaw, I'm bigger than you
Hey Chainsaw, I'm bigger than you
Hey Chainsaw, I'm bigger than you

Frustration, makes you do things
Frustration
Frustration, boogie man put a hex on you
Frustration
Bogady bogady whoo

Hey Chainsaw, I'm bigger than you
Hey Chainsaw, I'm bigger than you

Chainsaw in the song is a roadie of mine from my early career. He was a big,
gentle guy. We had a laugh together. I had to write a song about him.

I Love My Baby

My baby says to me
Come over here
And talk with me

I go and I sit down
We talk about the
Joy
We've found

I love my baby
I love my baby
So much

Love to hear you
Call my name
Out loud
Love to hear you
Say I make you proud

But will it end now
We can't say
Will we be happy
All the way

I love my baby
I love my baby
So much

Strange

Strange
How everything feels so strange
Since you walked out on me

I should be feeling blue
I should be feeling sad
But strange
So strange
I'm not crying over you

Strange how this space
Once too small
No room to breathe
Now overpowers me

Now I'm free to choose
I only see the walls
Closing in on me
So strange
So strange
I'm not missing you

When I was a girl
I dreamed about you
And for a while
You made my life a dream
But now it's all over
And it all seems so

Strange
How the real stories end
No happy ever after
No beginning again

Strange
So strange
So strange
I am not missing you

Talking to the Wall

There's a very old expression
Called
Talking to the wall
And it means
You get no answers
Just stone silence

But walls have ears
And you can hear me
When I call

I can feel it
Feel it
In my bones
You really mean it
It is not a hoax

Sham bam
Thank you ma'am
Not for you
You're bona fide . . . ah

You don't come on
In a Trojan horse
No hidden wires
To make me fall

What I see
Is what I get
Straight and true
My solid wall

You keep my chin up
Stabilise my highs and lows
You're extra-special
Nothing superficial

You see right through me
Rust
Cracks
Warts and all
Nothing changes
I'm the last word
In what you want

You're as solid
As a wall
And I can
Lean against you

I can tell you
All my troubles
And I know
You'll hear me

Walls have ears
You can hear me
When I call
Talking to the wall

Figure of Speech

He'll teach you to wait by the phone
And then won't call
Throw your life in a turmoil
And when you fall
Just when you need him most
He won't see you
Don't let him
Don't let him
Don't let him get you down

When your dreams get shattered
Down where nothing matters
But if he won't have you
You can bet your life
Bet your life
It's not the end
And if he can't see
What a friend you are
That's his loss
It's not the end

Don't let him
Don't let him
Don't let him get you down

Watch his lips while he speaks
And read his eyes
It's a figure of speech
So don't be surprised
When he talks of love
But his deeds can break you

Don't let him
Don't let him
Don't let him get you down

Kind Words and a Real Good Heart

Kind words and a real good heart
Doesn't mean you get respect
Kind words and a real good heart
Doesn't mean you get the best
It doesn't mean they won't get brutal
It doesn't mean they won't assault you
With a kind heart
With a kind heart

Bad guys sometime hard to find
'Cause they don't all dress in black
Good guys sometime make mistake
I say don't look
Don't look back
Be mindful how you get used up
You can't always
Trust an honest man
Be mindful how you get used up
You can't always
Trust an honest man

You gotta make your own beginning
Mark it down
Growing pains
With a kind heart
With a kind heart

Kind words and a real good heart
Doesn't mean you get respect
Kind words and a real good heart
Doesn't mean you get the best

It doesn't mean the whole world loves you
It doesn't mean more than it means
A kind heart
A kind heart

Kind words and a real good heart
Doesn't mean you get respect
Kind words and a real good heart
Doesn't mean you get the best

Reach Out

When the world has gone crazy
And there's no one around
You can talk to
I'll be there in a hurry
'Cause I know how you feel
Don't you worry

Reach out
I'll be there
Reach out for someone who cares
I'll be there
I'll make you feel fine
I'll put your mind at ease
I can be of help
I know I can
I can help

When you're looking for a friend
You won't find no better
Right on to the bitter end
Here I am
Here I am

When you feel a little bit lonely
There's no need
Can't you hear me

Reach out
I'll be there
Reach out for someone who cares
I'll be there

I will be the one
I'll make you feel fine
I can be the one to put your mind at ease
I can be of help I know I can
I can help

When you're looking for a friend
You won't find no better
Right on to the bitter end
Here I am
Here I am
Here I am

All a Woman Needs

Brings her flowers every day
And he phones her every night
Because she's his fancy
She's bound to love him too
And he's proved his feelings
He gives her all she needs
This boy can't understand

Though he holds her in his arms
He won't whisper words of love
He thinks it's alright
Love can come later

But woman
Love is all she needs
He will never get his way
With ease
He has to woo her properly
Or he'll never win her heart

Man likes to own
A woman shares
Man has his needs
A woman cares

Never means to make her cry
Oh he wants this girl so bad
The boy can't understand
He thinks it's alright
Love can come later

But woman
Love is all she needs
He will never get his way
With ease
He has to woo her properly
Or he'll never win her heart

'All a Woman Needs' is about a woman who just longs for her partner to say to her they love her. They will give her everything she wants, but what she wants most is to be told she is loved, and this is what her partner finds hard to say.

Dark Truths

I've told some dark truths
And I can't keep on lying
'Cause one day I'll find
I'm not your hero

It's so nice that someone thinks
You're special
Treat them right
That trust in you is precious
All the same
We make mistakes

I've used up a few lives
Now I'm afraid of dying
'Cause one day
I'll find
You're not forgiving

It's so nice
There's someone to rely on
Treat them right
That trust in you is precious
All the same
All the same
We make mistakes
And I've used up a few lives
Oh

The Devil I Know

Makes the call
Say everything's gonna be alright
Don't worry Joanie
I'll be a little bit late tonight
But I worry
'Cause I know
That's just how I got you

Likes a woman
That he has to chase a lot
So I worry
You know
It breaks a poor girl's heart
I know how he works
I know all the signs
I inspired the lines

Men
No self-control
Says I'm all he wants
But I watch him prowl
Yet if I should stray
I'm a wicked child
And he'd make me pay
The devil I know

One of these days
But that's what I always say
The devil I know

And the games that he can play
I know how he works
I know all the lines

Men
No self-control
But I watch him prowl
Yet if I should stray
I'm a wicked child
And he'd make me pay

The devil I know
The devil I know
One of these days
That's what I always say
But it's the devil I know
The games that he can play

The Shouting Stage

I thought we had it sweet
But your mind's played
A trick on me
I thought that I'd be with you
All the time
And I'd be fine
Yeah, I'd be fine

I'll swear you have my feelings
Under thought control
I know you've taken
Such a hold on me
I'm thinking more and more
Of what we had before

Before we lost it at the shouting stage
Before the days we'd sit there
Side by side
Without a word
And how that hurt

How could eternal love
Made above
We were so in love
We were joined up at the sides
How could two people
Be as one
As one
Blind from the same light
Be out of love with love
In no time

I thought we had it made
But my mind's played this trick on me
I thought that I would see you
All the time
And I'd be fine
Mmm I'd be fine

I swear you have no feelings
Or you'd call me home
I know there's no one else
There's no one else
Is there
I'm thinking more and more
Of what we had before
We lost it at the shouting stage
Before we lost it at the shouting stage

Free

Everything I try to give you
Everything I try to do
There's no pleasing you
You want the stars in the morning
And the sun dead of night
You place immovable objects
In my plain sight

Well I'm giving you your freedom
Though I never owned you
Nor wanted to
Hey hey hey hey

You're free
Now enjoy your freedom
Don't call me up
For cheap advice
You're free
Make your own decisions
You live your life
And let me live mine

Never held out on affection
Gave you most material things
There's no pleasing you
You called me your lover
Did I treat you that bad
You really want me to suffer
But I can take so much

Well I'm giving you your freedom
Though I never owned you
Nor wanted to
Hey hey hey hey

You're free
Now enjoy your freedom
Don't call me up
For cheap advice
You're free
Make your own decisions
You live your life
And let me live mine
Please

More Than One Kind of Love

There's a lot of things you should hold dear
Keep in your heart
Never let go
Never let go
Never let go
Pride and dignity
A sense of self
Hold on

When that boy leaves
And you need someone to turn to
When you feel alone
You will know you're not alone
If you've been true
To all who are true to you
You'll make it
You'll make it fine

If you remember your friends
Just remember you can call
Just remember that passion fades
Good friendships seldom die
Go ahead have your fun
But don't turn your back on everyone
Though the body needs love
There is more than one kind

More
More than one kind of love
There is more
More than one kind

Yes he fills your heart
Fills your mind
He's all you want
All you need
Everything
Everything
Everything but

Love that's that exclusive
That obsessive
Can hurt

When that love pales
And becomes human emotion
Where will you go
If you've neglected those you know
But if you stay true
To those who are true to you
You'll make it
You'll make it fine

If you remember your friends
Just remember you can call
Just remember that passion fades
Good friendships seldom die
Go ahead have your fun
But don't turn your back on everyone
Though the body needs love
There is more than one kind

More
More than one kind of love
There is more
More than one kind

The Power of Dreams

Somehow you supply
All of the answers
I've fallen for your lack of mystery
Your honest emotions
Your love for me
Has opened up my world
Renewed my taste for life
Nothing was easy
Till you

You came
Everything else just fell into place
Till you
Daily routine was dragging me down

But somewhere deep inside
All disillusions
Were shattered by your hand touching mine
The strength of a new love
Can conquer
All
I ever want is here
By any other name
The power of love

You came
Everything else just fell into place
You made all of the bad times
Just disappear
My step is light
You made my soul and my spirits fly

And how my fortune changed
The power of change

All I ask of all my hopes
My one recurring dream
The power of dreams
The power of dreams

Promise Land

All this time I have followed the rules
And I've lived the perfect life
Alright
By somebody else's standards
All this time I did not feel too bad
But I was not what you call happy
Not really
I was searching for something
And all this time you were standing by
And all this time you were waiting

All this time I've been living a lie
And I even fooled myself completely
Now I'm really ready
Right or wrong
I will follow your course
And if you go down I'll drown
So save me
I'm not as strong as I look
Yeah
All this time I've been saying
No
But all this time
I've been meaning

Yes I'm ready to take your hand
Follow you into the promise land
Ooh yeah let's talk about it
I'm a fool for you
Ducking and diving
'Cause I'm a fool for you

All this time I've been saying
No
But all this time
I've been meaning
Yes I'm ready to take your hand
Follow you into the promise land

Someone's in the Background

Someone's in the background
While we're on the phone
Giving you the answers
Where do they get
All this information
And how

Put 'em on the phone right now
I want to pick their brains tonight
They can tell me where I'm going wrong
They can tell me how to make love

Put 'em on the phone right now
I want to talk to the stealer
They can tell me how they hurt inside
Because they know how much I'm hurting
They can say that when a good love dies
I'll find some comfort in my memories

Someone made you question
The love we had
The love we had
Should have lasted a thousand years
You've been persuaded that was way too long
Put 'em on the phone right now
I want to talk to the person
Who taught you how to spread your wings

Communication breakdown
I thought you cared
I thought you cared

When did we get to this position
And how
Tell me on the phone right now
You're going to sleep on your own tonight
I can find you out in a lie
You can't disguise the passion

I'm coming round there now
I want to see this angel
Once you're caught
Then there's no turning back
Like a rat you won't escape the trap

Tell me on the phone right now
You're going to sleep on your own tonight
I can find you out in a lie
You can't disguise the passion
And you can say that now our love has died
I'll find some comfort in my memories

Something in the Air Tonight

It's like I'm in a movie
And I'm the villain of the piece
You're some sweet angel child
Even strangers blame me
While you come up smelling sweet
How come I'm always cast in all the tragedies

I can remember when
We used to talk of getting old
We'd act our parts and roll with laughter
On the floor

Well we're not acting now
It's cold it's as a war
You shut me out
Where once you'd open every door
This could make comedy
If it wasn't for the tragedy
How could you hide
Your love away from me

You can't really hate me
Though you've said it once before
But there's something in the air tonight
I can remember when
We used to talk

I can remember when
We used to talk of getting old
We'd act our parts and roll with laughter
On the floor

[92]

This could make comedy
If it wasn't for the tragedy
How could you hide
Your love away from me

Can't Get Over How I Broke Your Heart

Tried to do the best for you
Things I said
Were meant to last
Loved you so
I hate to go
I feel strong with you

I know I deserve this
If I could change the hands of time
Turn back the page

I can't get over
How I broke your heart
And the moment
That I lost my pride
And I can't forget
That look in your eyes
You were begging me
Don't make you cry
Loved you so
I almost said
I was home alone
But I couldn't see you more hurt
When you found out the lie

Not your fault
Not your fault
I know I've deceived you
I let my head be ruled
While my conscience told me

If I get caught
Our love will end
I didn't seem to care

Now I can't get over
How I broke your heart
And the moment
That I lost my pride
And I can't forget
That look in your eyes
You were begging me
Don't make you cry
Now I can't get over
How I tore my whole world apart

I can't get over
How I broke your heart
And the moment
And I can't forget
That look in your eyes
You were begging me

Love you so I always will
Though you're miles from me
And I can't get over
How I tore my whole world apart

I can't get over
How I broke your heart
And the moment
And I can't forget
That look in your eyes
You were begging me

I can't get over
How I broke your heart
And the moment
That I lost my pride
And I can't forget
That look in your eyes
You were begging me
Don't make you cry

Cradled in Your Love

What was so special
We were exact
So much together
We were like that
You'd send chills down my spine
Or burn me up
With your desire

What happened to you and me
And the love that we once knew

I read the letters
I found the cards
Not hidden well
I thought love
Transcended lust
I guess my heart was wishing

What happened to you and me
And the love that we once knew
You never said it would end
And I thought we were unique

Safe and sound
Cradled in your love

What happened to you and me
And the love that we once knew
You never said it would end
And I thought we were unique

You never said it would end
And I thought I could depend
On a lifetime
Spent with you

Crazy

I don't mind if you tell me
That you're never coming back no more
Don't mind if you say
A dozen women got babies
And they're all yours
Don't mind if you tell me
That you got to work late tonight
No matter what you're saying
As long as you say it while

You hold me in your arms
Squeeze me nice and tight
Let's get down to business
I hear you speak
But my lips still seek your kisses
I know I'm crazy

There's women who want you for your money
Well they get what they deserve
May you never
Reach rock bottom babe
But I'd be there
With some extra fine clothes
So you can

Take me on the town
Flaunt our love around
Dancing rude
We're gonna leave
'Cause the steam will start a hissin'
You drive me crazy

Let me
Hold you in my arms
Hug your breath away
Let's get down to business
My younger days
Must have lacked some supervision
You lead me astray

Me myself and I want you
I know you're a lover who can't be true
I'm lucky that I got you
To show me love and affection
Tonight
Let's get down to business
I hear you speak
But my lips still seek your kisses
I know I'm crazy

Hold me in your arms
Squeeze me nice and tight
Let's get down to business
I hear you speak
But my lips still seek your kisses
Drive me crazy

Sometimes I Don't Wanna Go Home

Shell me with questions all night
I'm living in a danger zone
Like a sword of destruction
Eating at your very soul

Possessed by emotional ties
Your love is a chain
Ooh hoo hoo

Sometimes I don't wanna go home
'Cause I know it's gonna start again
Sometimes I don't wanna go home
'Cause I know it's gonna start again

I'm the soul of discretion
Your mountain is a grain of sand
And I'm tired of the life that I live
Ruled by your iron hand

Stop picking on me
It's getting down from bad to worse
Stop picking on me

Is this love
Is this love
Is this love
Is this love

Sometimes I don't wanna go home
'Cause I know it's gonna start again

Sometimes I don't wanna go home
'Cause I know it's gonna start again

Shell me with questions all night
I'm living in a danger zone
Obsessed and emotional
Your love is a chain

Sometimes I don't wanna go home
Sometimes I don't wanna go home

Sometimes I don't wanna go home
'Cause I know it's gonna start again
Sometimes I don't wanna go home
'Cause I know it's gonna start again

Square the Circle

You lean your back against the wall
Push your hands in your pocket
You look down

Pacing the floor
You look out the window
Beyond the view

Shake your body
As if against the cold
Your mind wanders

Tell me what you're trying to say
Tell me what you're trying to say
I won't stop
Loving you

We sit down together
You start to draw a ring
Square the circle
Then draw some lines

Push the paper
But keep the pen you hold
You need your hands occupied

Tell me what you're trying to say
Tell me what you're trying to say
I won't stop
I won't stop
Loving you

Let your fingers intertwine
Put your hands behind your head
Lean back
And close your eyes
And tell me

Tell me
What you've got on your mind
Tell me
Tell me

Everyday Boy

Well I've never met anyone
With your courage
And the way you enjoy life
Puts me to shame
Just an hour with you
And I understand
Why we had to meet

I saw you look in the mirror
And adjust your hair
Smile and leave the room

Just an everyday boy
Doing everyday things
But you're somebody special
Somebody who feels
You're not the first
And you won't be the last
But you are the one
I'll remember

It's God's revenge
You're surrounded by fear
A compassionate man
You hold people dear
No blame for the mother
Who curses your name
She fears for her son
It's death by association

But you respect yourself
And you let it show
Some fade with guilt
And the shame
The way you
Tell your story
With no tears
For yourself

Just an everyday boy
Doing everyday things
You're not the first
And you won't be the last
But you are the one
I'll remember

Hey hey
Just an everyday boy
Just an everyday boy

Doing everyday things
Just an everyday boy
Just an everyday boy
Just an everyday boy
Doing everyday things
Just an everyday boy

'Everyday Boy' is about someone who had AIDS. He told me the story of
his boyfriend's mother who disliked him because she thought her son would
automatically die because they were together. He was so sympathetic to his
boyfriend's mother's position. I thought he was one of the kindest people I
have ever met.

Lost the Love

Baby's gone
Baby's gone and left me
I'm so sorry
I'm so sorry for the thing

I wouldn't blame you
If you never come back
Darling what you had to go through
I could never live like that
I was stupid stupid stupid
I'm ashamed

I lost the friends we made
I lost the money we saved
I lost the love you gave
In the early days
I had everything
Threw it all away
Threw it all away
I was mad

Darling I've changed
You have my word on that
I was a fool to myself
And a devil to you
How I hurt you really hurt me
Ashamed
I miss the fun we had
I miss the games we played
I knew the score
Still I cheated

Now I'm history
Threw it all away
Threw it all away
I was mad
I was mad
I was mad

I lost the friends we made
I lost the money we saved
I lost the love you gave
In the early days
I had everything
Couldn't ask for more
Threw it all away
It's so sad
I was bad
I was mad

I lost a precious thing
Respect from you
I blew it all
Now I want it back
It's good news day
When you call me up
Please won't you call me
I'll be good

Merchant of Love

You're selling emotions
That I can't buy
Don't want the sadness
Price is far too high
And I don't want
I don't need your packaged lies
I've got too much in store

Someone help me
Find the merchant of love
Selling heaven here on earth
I've bought pain and measures
Of pure heartache
I've had all I can take

I'm willing to wait
For lasting pleasure
With promises
That won't ever break
Someone help me
Find the merchant of love
With a full guarantee

I'd travel
Miles and miles and miles
To find the place
With treasures
Much more rich than gold
I just want a heart
That captures my soul
And I'm willing to wait

I'm willing to wait
For lasting pleasure
With promises
That won't ever break
Someone help me
Find the merchant of love

Someone help me
Find the merchant of love
With a full guarantee

Trouble

You've lived your life
And how you survived
I'll never know
People talk of hardships
What do they know
What do they know
Of the strength you had to show

To stop yourself from crying out
To keep your head above the sand
Those times when you were in despair
When trouble seemed your only friend
Somehow you kept your spirits high
You told him straight
Don't call again

Now there were times
When it seemed I didn't care
Don't misjudge my silence
You had my sympathy
I had sympathy
And I admired how you

Stopped yourself from crying
Kept your head above the sand
When trouble seemed your only friend
Somehow you kept your spirits high
You told him straight
Don't call again

And now the future's looking bright
You fought alone and won the fight
Kept your faith
When times were hard you made it through
Trouble seemed your only friend
Somehow you kept your spirits high

You stopped yourself from crying out
You kept your head above the sand
Those times when you were in despair
Trouble seemed your only friend
Somehow you kept your spirits high
You told him straight
Don't call again

The Messenger

Nelson
People love you
'Cause your message is strong
So let's raise our voices
Let's raise our voices
Let's sing to the messenger

The message
That you delivered
Told us how we should be
We should treat each other
As we would be treated
Oooh, oooh, oooh

You are admired for your enviable strength
The forgiving heart you showed to the world
You faced the demons of oppression with grace
Freed a nation through unparalleled love
Now your celebratory moon has risen
Your name will live on in history
With many more you fought for the freedom
That's given like breath at the time of our birth

Yeah Madiba
Madiba
Mandela

Nelson
People love you
'Cause your message is strong
So let's raise our voices

Let's raise our voices
Let's sing to the messenger

Yeah
People love you
'Cause your message is strong
So let's raise our voices
Let's raise our voices
Let's sing to the messenger

The pimpernel
A saint or an icon
Whatever name is given to you
You bear each one with great humility
But Nelson Mandela says all about you

Yeah Madiba
Madiba
Mandela

I was asked to write a song for Nelson Mandela and I was lucky enough to play it for him at a private function he had in London in 2001. I recorded the song with the Kingdom Choir and asked them to perform it with me when I sang it for him. He loved the song and danced all the way through it, and gave me a massive hug at the end of it.

Blessed

Life is hard
Work is dirty
Friends plead poverty
Fame and fortune
Keeps its own time
So don't wait up

But if you can feel the sun
If you can feel the rain
Life can't be bad
If you've got food to eat
And all your dreams to dream
Life can't be bad
If you can walk away
And fight another day
Life can't be that bad

For all the things that I can do
How could I complain
I've got no broken wings
I've got a heart that sings
And I feel blessed

Crazy for You

I wanted you when and I want you now
And I always will
I wanted the best
And you are the best
Please don't leave

I don't want you to go
I'm a fool for you baby
I just want you to know
I'm a fool for you baby

Talked with a friend
We were up all night
We were looking at words
I searched for the ones
That would change your mind
Please

I just want you to know
I'm a fool for you baby
I just want you to know
I'm a fool for you baby

In this strange and troubled world
In this strange and troubled world

In this strange and troubled world
I just lost my mind
Let's clean the slate and start again
Don't leave me unforgiven

And I want you to know
My life is in your hands
I just want you to know
It's only you

I wasn't looking for someone else
And even at intimate times I felt
Like I was watching another life
In another world
In another time
And all the while my heart was crying
Crying like a little child
'Cause all I wanted was you so much
But I just couldn't help myself

And I want you to know
You have the smile that I'm after
I just want you to know
I'm crazy, crazy
For you
For your laughter
For your love

Fire and Ice

I don't wanna know everything
About you
Can't love everything everything
That you do

No baby don't wanna find anybody else
Nobody could ever find another lover
Never find another lover like you
Like oil and water we don't mix
But something keeps us tied together

We fight
Fire and ice
Black is white
Night is day
That's how we treat each other

But I don't wanna go anywhere
Without you
I could never find
Loving as tempestuous

You say hot
I say cold
But oh when the fight is over
You say yes
I say yes
And we dive underneath the covers

And I don't wanna go anywhere
Without you

I don't wanna go anywhere
Without you
I don't wanna I don't wanna go anywhere
Without you

I say left
You say right
Before the night is over
I say yes
You say yes
And we dive underneath the covers

I don't wanna go anywhere
Without you
I don't wanna go anywhere
Without you

No baby don't wanna find anybody else
Never find another lover
Not another lover ever gonna make me happy
Like you make me happy
You make me happy
You make me happy

In These Times

These are the times
Tears fill the back of your eyes
These are the times
The birds migrate
Across the skies

These are the times
What hope you had you forget
These wicked times
You're bound to feel
All sanity is lost

In these times everyone needs love
In these times do you pray to God
In these times everyone needs comfort
And would welcome a hand to hold
Compassion is the fire
That burns the hurt
That pains the soul
And though my eyes are so polluted
By the sight of lost desires
I can see you standing by

This is my fear
That distance will come between us
And it could mean nothing
Nothing
To get from here to there

We own the world
And everything that's in it

Let our love shine
Like glistening raindrops
Resting on a rose

In these times celebrate our love
In these times let's be thankful of
All the days we can spend together
And I'm happy to hold your hand
Your passion is the food
That feeds the hunger in my heart
And now my eyes are clearly open
No more longing for the past
Now I have you in these times

In these times everyone needs love
In these times do you pray to God
In these times everyone needs comfort
And would welcome a hand to hold
Your passion is the fire
That burns the hurt
That pains the soul
And though my eyes are so polluted
By the sight of lost desires
Good to have you in these times

I wrote 'In These Times' after watching a mother and father talk about their
son going off to war. The mother was distraught. She was crying and afraid
that she would never see her son again after he went to serve. The father on
the other hand was proud that his son was going off to fight. I was struck by
the opposing reactions and emotions of the parents.

Less Happy More Often

Once in a while
We share a thought
But most of all we drift apart
Haven't you noticed
We seem less happy more often

And I don't know what to do
Whether to be with you
And I'm as sure as sure
I can't live without you
So what is to become of us
How do we get it back
I'm as certain as you
That I don't like it

When we embrace
The thrill is gone
But in reality we hardly touch at all
Haven't you noticed
We get more lonely
More often

And I don't know what to do
Whether to be with you
And I'm as sure as sure I'm sure
I can't live without you
So what is to become of us
Where do we go from here
I'm as upset as you
At how our love has gone

When we began
We shared a dream
And all our strength was in our unity
Haven't you noticed we seem less mighty
More helpless

I don't know what to do
I can't put the blame on you
But I can't blame myself
So it's neutral
So what is to become of us
How do we get it back
I'm as desperate as you
To be in love again

Let's Talk About Us

Let's sit down
Let's have a nice long talk about us
You start

Let's go out
Let's walk down the street
We'll fool around
Walking on the kerb
Walking on the kerb

I've always wanted you
I dreamed of you at night
I couldn't see your face
But I knew you were the one

Right from the start
You treated me just the way you should
I've always wanted you
I dreamed of you at night
I couldn't see your face
But I knew you were the one
I knew you were the one

Good things happening for us all the time
Good things happening for us all the time

Every day I get a little sunshine
Even though the day's a rainy day
Every day you give me all your loving
And I thank you

Romance me
Sweet-talk me
Send me weak at the knees
Let's dance around the room

I've always wanted you
I dreamed of you at night
I couldn't see your face
But I knew you were the one

Good things happening for us all the time
Good things happening for us all the time
Every day I get a little sunshine
Even though the day's a rainy day
Every day you give me all your loving
And I thank you

Good things are happening for us all the time

Love Bug

It may rain tomorrow
But tonight is all that's on my mind
My baby's here
In my arms
You know we've got it bad
'Cause tonight we've got the love virus

We've both come down with the love bug
And it means we've got to stay in bed
I hope yous guys don't catch this
'Cause it knocks you right off a your legs

Love bug
Talking 'bout love bug
I said love bug
You know I mean love bug

Let me splain the symptoms
First of all there's hardly any pain
With the love bug
You kind of lose you memory
You see
Hear
Think
Talk
Dream
Care
Just for one person
Only

Don't come down with the love bug
'Cause it drives the sense
Right out of your head

This thing strikes in a curious way
It only hits when you're not looking

Don't stand close to anybody
Who'll contaminate you
If you come down with the virus
Well you'll never be alone again

We've both come down with the love bug
And it means we've got to stay in bed
I hope yous guys don't catch this
'Cause it knocks you right off a your legs

Love bug
Talking 'bout love bug
I said love bug
You know I mean love bug
I said love bug

Talking 'bout love bug
Yeah love bug
You know I mean love bug
Yeah love bug
Talking 'bout love bug
Yeah love bug

Lovers' Speak

When they whisper in the corner
When they're running in the rain
When they're holding hands and laughing
Tell me what they're really saying

Lovers' speak is so much different
Only they can understand
Let's all share this coded secret
Let us in let's all join hands
Lovers walk a different tightrope
Lovers always speak in tongues

I wanna learn the language of love
I wanna learn how to flirt
I wanna hear someone call out my name
And wipe away all the hurt

When they're reckless with abandon
Nothing can get in their way
There's no natural disaster
Could dull their senses
Stop their play

Lovers' world is so much different
Make me a native of that land
Let's all share this special feeling
That lifts you up beyond the heavens
Lovers walk a looser tightrope
With feathers thrown upon the ground

I wanna count all those blessings I'll get
When I gaze on that face
Who'll glamorise all my fantasies more
I tell you now I can't wait

I wanna learn the language of love
I wanna learn how to flirt
I wanna hear someone call out my name
And wipe away all the hurt

Lovers speaking
Lovers speaking
Everyone will listen
Everyone will listen
Everyone wants to learn

They wanna learn the language of love
They wanna learn how to flirt
They wanna hear someone call out their name
And wipe away all the hurt

I wanna learn lovers' speak
I wanna learn lovers' speak

I wanna learn the language of love
I wanna learn how to flirt
I wanna hear someone call out my name
And wipe away all the hurt

Ocean

I've got to keep on keeping on
I just wanna be beside you
Wanna do the best I can
Even though you've made it plain
You don't believe in love
I can't let you go
I can't walk away

Come on baby, can't you see
All the need in me
Like the ocean speaks to the naked man
The rhythm of your heart is like a sonnet
Pure and sweet
How you haunt my memory

Believe me baby
In this brilliant world you're the best
You're like a porcelain charm
A perfumed smile
A teenage blush
You're like champagne roses

Come on baby, can't you see
All the need in me
Like the ocean speaks to the naked man

I've got to keep on keeping on
How can I live without you
I've got to make you understand
Each species has a mate

And fate says you'll be mine
I won't let you down

Come on baby, can't you see
All the need in me
Like the ocean speaks to the naked man
The rhythm of your heart is like a sonnet
Pure and sweet
How you haunt my memory

I believe in angels
You leave me no alternative
You're like a butterfly
A gospel choir
A sun-kissed sky
You're like sensual velvet

Believe me baby
In this brilliant world you're the best
You're like a porcelain charm
A perfumed smile
A teenage blush
You're like sunshine roses

Come on baby, can't you see
All the need in me
Like the ocean speaks to the naked man

Physical Pain

It's a physical pain
My head just aches
I'm feeling raw
I feel crucified
I don't feel great

I'm gonna lick my wounds
Hide my crying eyes
It's my own fault
I told you lies

No touch sensation
No palpitations
Don't lick my lips
Don't lick my lips
In anticipation

I'm traumatised
And I feel confined
I seem so unsettled
I don't feel alive

I'm gonna lick my wounds
Hide my crying eyes
It's my own fault
I told you lies

No excitations
No good vibrations
Just a physical pain
Just a physical pain

Will I ever get to see you darling
This broken friendship
Means my broken heart
Are we ever gonna get together
Will I ever see your smiling face again
Can't wait

There's too much space
These empty rooms
Time on my hands
I'm gonna lick my wounds
Hide my crying eyes
It's my own fault
I told you lies
No excitations, no good vibrations
It's solitaire

I feel lost
I feel alone
With no desire
I feel numb

Will I ever get to see you darling
This broken friendship
Means my broken heart
Are we ever gonna get together
Will I ever see your smiling face again
Are we ever gonna get together
Are we ever gonna get together

Prove Yourself

Some things are gonna come easy
Some things are gonna be hard
But don't let them put you off your stride
'Cause you could make your mark

You're gonna get married
You're gonna be rich
Your gonna have all the things you ever wished
You're gonna be the boss
You know you're gonna pull
You could be the saviour of this wicked world

Sometimes you gotta be smarter
You've got to play to win the game
Don't let them make you give up
Right before you can begin

Going to the moon
Win a peace prize
Discover there's life on the other side
You're gonna get slim
Make a new friend
You can do whatever you think you can

People are gonna wanna tell you
Don't try too much
They're gonna warn you
About disappointment but

You're gonna prove yourself
You're gonna prove yourself

You're gonna prove yourself
You're gonna prove yourself

You're gonna tour the world
You're gonna write a book
You could be the one who finds life on Mars
You're gonna be happy
Listen to the voice
You can do it right
If you make that choice

To prove yourself
You're gonna prove yourself
You're gonna prove yourself
You're gonna prove yourself

You can do anything
You can do anything
You can do anything

You can do anything
You can do anything
You can do anything

And you're gonna prove yourself
You can prove yourself

A Woman in Love

When the morning comes
Like shifting sands
In a desert storm
Like a raging fire
Heats up the big sky baby
Your love is pure and strong
Chained to your heart I surrender
Here's where I belong

And if I get emotional and I'm restless
You're like a soothing ray of light
Bring me to my senses in a heartbeat darling
Hold me tender in the night

Tell me what miracles are made of
Like the sweet soft morning dew
How can I ever show you baby
How can I prove it all to you

That I'm a woman in love
I'm a woman in love
I'm a woman in love
I'm a woman in love

I get so mixed up and tongue-tied
I can hardly say my name
Bring me to my senses in a heartbeat darling
Hold me tender in the night

'Cause I'm a woman in love
I'm a woman in love

I'm a woman in love
I'm a woman in love

Never thought this would
Never thought this would
Never thought this would happen to me

Never thought this would
Never thought this would
Never thought this would happen to me

I'm a woman in love
I'm a woman in love
I'm a woman in love
I'm a woman in love

DNA

Please sit down
Tell me what you got to say
Now there's a difference between truth and lies
I can check
I've got your DNA
Now look me right between the eyes
Tell me when I saw you
And your new lady friend
What were you talking about
When you laughed
And your two cheeks met
What were you talking about

Let us talk
In the morning babe
I've got your DNA and the lie detect
How I thought I could change you babe
All those flies buzzing round your head

Look at me
There's nothing new over there
You've seen that stereo a thousand times
Lift your head
And lift my spirits up
Because you know
I'm dying deep inside
Don't you care about me
Are you looking for freedom
Is that what you're thinking about
Do you wanna hold me in your arms and kiss
'Cause that's what I'm thinking about

Let us talk
In the morning babe
I've got your DNA and the lie detect
How I thought I could change your ways
All those flies buzzing round your head

You got a brand-new way of loving
Keeping the lights turned on
You keep a comb in your pocket
And your shiny shiny shoes
Yeah don't touch the ground these days
What's going on
Yeah you think I'm stupid 'cause I don't complain
Better sit yourself down start talking fast
And if the lying don't kill you
The truth just might make you fade away
Fade away
Fade away

Empty Highway

Watch the rain gently fall
Like the tears running down my face

Watch the rain gently fall
Like the tears running down my face

Sometimes it feels like the sky is violence
Sometimes it feels like nobody cares
Sometimes it feels like I'm on an empty highway
And I'm on a road to nowhere
I'm on a road to nowhere

As I watch the street lights flicker
Like the dying embers of your affection

As I watch the street lights flicker
Like the dying embers of your affection

Sometimes it feels like we never kissed
I've got no interest in the push and pull of the tides
Who cares if the world stops spinning
'Cause I'm a lonely number
Yeah I'm a lonely number

As I lay me down to sleep
All the little birds and the bees
That would sing to all the lovers
They just pass me by
Yeah
Yeah
Yeah

Even in my dreams
Vivid colours turn to a grey scale

Even in my dreams
Vivid colours turn to a grey scale

And I turn to you and I ask
How can I make things better
And you say it's gone it's gone it's gone it's over
And I stand outside in just my underwear
And I watch the gentle rain fall
Yeah watch the gentle rain fall down
Yeah I watch the gentle rain fall down

Heading Back to New York City

Going back to New York City
To do the things I never did

I'm heading back to New York City
To see the things I never saw

Things like the ABC No Rio, oh oh
I'm gonna search this town both high and low
I'm gonna go all the places where New Yorkers go
I'm gonna see Staten Island, gonna take the boat
I'm gonna search every place till I reach zero

Going back to New York City
You might be by those Asian trees
I'm heading back to New York City
Times Square and all those Broadway babes

And if the devil has a playground, yeah yeah
You wanna bet New York is the devil's swing
Let's shake, let's make a deal
Of all the bright-light cities spread around the globe
There ain't a skyline better than New York, New York

I'm going back to the place I lost my heart
I'm going back to the place I lost my heart
Spend my time trying to find you
Here in New York

Going back to New York City
To do the things I never did
I know I'm gonna find you baby, yeah yeah

I'm gonna search this town both high and low
I'm gonna go all the places where New Yorkers go
I'm gonna see Staten Island, gonna take the boat
I'm gonna search every place till I reach zero

I'm going back to New York City
Heading back to find you

I'm going back to New York City
Heading back to find you

Into the Blues

My baby likes this music good and loud
With words coming straight from the heart
Man woman or child can tell this story
Just as long as it's a soulful start
All the better to make you glad
That your life has taken a different path
At the same time wondering
How you can get on a train
To this town

My baby don't like rock and roll
Not hip-hop or pop
My baby's just into the blues
My baby's just into the blues
My baby's just into the blues
My baby's just into the blues

God bless the blues
God bless the blues
Hey yeah
Are you a mannish boy
Just like the mighty Mud
Blues are here to make you glad
That your life has taken a different path
At the same time wondering
How you can get on a train
To this town

My baby don't like rock and roll
Not hip-hop or pop
My baby's just into the blues

My baby's just into the blues
My baby's just into the blues
My baby's just into the blues

My baby don't like rock and roll
Not hip-hop or pop
Dance might be real cool
And country's just for fools
Baroque is just for the old
For the tired and the restless souls
Lost in the darkness
Lost in the darkness

My baby's just into the blues
My baby's just into the blues
My baby's just into the blues
My baby's just into the blues

Liza

I see you looking at me
I know we're from different sides of town
You've never travelled
And I've been all around
Hey
Let me take your hand
Hey hey yeah
From where I stand
You're in need of a friend
So let the good times roll
Let the good times roll

I see something in you
I see it, how come they don't
You're a good person
And they'll come around
Hey
Let me take your hand
Hey hey yeah yeah
I can see you change
You're in need of a friend
So let the good times roll
Let the good times roll
Let the good times roll
Let the good times roll

Everybody says
Don't hang around with Liza
She's from the other side of town
The part where folks live on welfare
The part where you find needles on the ground

It's the side where the kids hang out in gangs
And wear the hoodies
And the masks
To hide their face
If you make friends with a girl like that
Well it's a big disgrace

Everybody say
This that
This that
This that
This that

Hey Liza
I'd like a friend like you
Hey Liza
I think you're kind of cute
Hey Liza
I'm gonna make up my own mind
I'm gonna make up my own mind

I see you looking at me
I know we're from different sides of town
You've never travelled
And I've been all around
Hey Liza
Let me take your hand
Hey hey yeah yeah
Yeah yeah yeah
From where I stand
You're in need of a friend
So let the good times roll
Let the good times roll
Let the good times roll
Let the good times roll

Mama Papa

I was born on an island
St Kitts
In a little biddy town
Had a mama and a papa
Four brothers and a sister

Mama Papa told us
Play hard
Fight fair
Live life
And love the Lord
I said love the Lord
Said love the Lord

Their choice was
The United Kingdom
Living in Birmingham
When they wanted to spread their wings and fly away

Seven people in one room
No heat
One wage
And bills to pay
I said bills to pay
Gotta pay those bills

Now when you're walking on heaven's floor
Talking in the ear of God
What you gonna say to the man
When he asks you what you've done

Can you say you did your very best
With what you had
Like my mama and my papa

I know two people who served up love
And a whole lot more
They made us hold our sides with laughter all night long
Oh they made us laugh
Until we cried
Till we begged them stop
Or we'll split our sides

Now when you're walking on heaven's floor
Talking in the ear of God
What you gonna say to the man
When he asks you what you've done

Can you say you did your very best
With what you had
Like my mama and my papa

Play the Blues

Blue hat
Checked shirt
Pimple on your cheek
Ears like handlebars
Teeth yellow
Like the sun
Gravelled voice like a beaten path
But baby when you sing the blues
I'd take all my clothes off for you
Baby when you sing the blues
I'd take all my clothes off for you

Wake up
Every day
Turn my face
To feel the morning breeze
At night
When we meet
You're brighter than a constellation of stars
Baby when you sing the blues
I'd take all my clothes off for you
Baby when you sing the blues
I'd take all my clothes off for you

Got a feeling that my cares gonna walk away
Got a feeling that my cares gonna walk away
Got a feeling that my cares gonna walk away
As long as baby don't leave
I'm happy every day

Secular Songs

They're singing secular songs in the churches
And there's not a word of God
It's all Schubert and Beethoven
Oh and lots of French love songs
So let's go down on Sunday morning
To hear that Jacob sermon read
Everybody dressed in their finest apparel baby
Listening to the preacher eulogise

Then we'll pray
Pray
Pray
Yeah we'll pray
Our souls will rise upon that day
Pray
Pray
Pray
Pray we change to better ways

They're telling stories about love's passion
All about *ménage à trois*
Hear those heartfelt lieder
Coming from that deep bass voice
And whilst some sleep through this music
Others weep for all the pain
As they sing secular songs in the churches baby
It's time to kneel, let's kneel and pray

Yeah we'll pray
Pray
Pray

Pray
Yeah we'll pray
Pray
Pray
Pray
Our souls will rise upon that day
Hallelujah
Hallelujah
Hallelujah
Pray we change to better ways

Yeah we'll pray
Pray
Pray
Pray
Pray
Pray
Pray we change

Something's Gotta Blow

Smell of a man
Smell of musk
The noise of the train
From morning till dusk
The up escalator broken down
The clothes on my back
Look like they were taken out of the laundry basket
Too weary to wash
Too weary to wash

Now there's hordes of people
Pushing and shoving
Sizzling noises coming out of their ears
Hold on to the strap
Or hold on to a stranger
Hope that stranger's day has not been too hard

Aggression builds up
When the going is slow
And you're packed like sardines
Something's gotta blow

Something's gotta blow
When you work so hard
And the sweat pours down on you
Something's gotta blow
When your pay don't match
The work you slave
And the pain you get

Something's gotta blow
Please stand on the right
So I can pass on the left
'Cause something's gotta blow
Something's gotta blow
Something's gotta blow

Dodging the fare
Ain't worth the crime
Think of your loved ones
Whilst you're doing your time
Being met at the station
Ain't no better thrill
Than that 4 × 4 cruiser
Coming over the hill
Bringing love and relief
From the noise and the heat
From the suicide jumpers
From that head nodding sleep

From the smell of burgers
And the rustling of sweets
Someone lend me your phone
So I can say which train to meet
Let me say which train to meet

Something's gotta blow
When you work so hard
And the sweat pours down on you
Something's gotta blow
When your pay don't match
The work you slave
And the pain you get

Something's gotta blow
Please stand on the right
So I can pass on the left
'Cause something's gotta blow
Something's gotta blow

Cry

I find myself
In times of trouble
And all I can do is cry

I find that all
The cares surround me
And all I can do
Is cry

Nothing you can do
Is ever gonna hurt like this
Nothing you can say
Is ever gonna hurt like this

I can't forget the one
Said I can't forget the one
No I can't forget the one
I saw you holding

As your beautiful mouth
Kissed those pouting lips
I could tell that I was losing

My source of comfort is now fading
And all I can do
Is cry

Nothing you can do
Is ever gonna hurt like this
Nothing you can say
Is ever gonna hurt like this

And I can't forget the one
I just can't forget the one
Said I can't forget the one
No I can't forget the one
I saw you holding

Why just doesn't matter
What I want to know is when

When did you stop craving
For the nearness of me
And my perfumed smell
When I play with your hair
And the feeling you get
When I touch you

The sun has set
Our love
Is shaded
And all I can do
Is cry

Nothing you can do
Is ever gonna hurt like this
Nothing you can say
Is ever gonna hurt like this

Goddess of Change

I was looking for the sunshine
For the bright side
To those gloomy clouds of steely grey

It all rests on this
How do I see things now
In my average day
Am I an average Joe
Or do I seize the moment
And call on Oya
The goddess of change

Oh my
It's funny how things turn out fine
Worries
They always seem much worse at night

It all rests on this
How do I see things now
In my average day
Am I an average Joe
Or do I seize the moment
And call on Oya
The goddess of change

Seeing lovers embrace
Makes you want to find your
Corner of happiness
Call the goddess Oya

Everybody looking for
Something to make them
Much more happy and
Somewhat sweeter than
Seize the moment
Call on Oya

People Who Win

I got a feeling in my bones
Everything is gonna work out

On a spiritual level
There ain't no mountain
That we can't climb

Let's go
Eh oh eh
Let's go
Eh oh eh
Let's go
Eh oh eh
Let's go
Eh oh eh

There is something going round
Trying to make our lives a wasteland

Put a stranglehold on hope
But there ain't no tempo we can't play

Let's go
Eh oh eh
Let's go
Eh oh eh
Let's go
Eh oh eh
Let's go
Eh oh eh

Everybody gets to ride a bad patch of life
But it don't mean luck is never on your side
There's a bad man trying to break our backs
But he'll need the strength of ten before he breaks a sweat

We're fierce like a lion
Strong in our convictions
Hey we are determined in our heart and soul

Yeah we stand
Yeah we fight
Yeah we hold
Into the night

Let's go
Eh oh eh
Let's go
Eh oh eh
Let's go
Eh oh eh
Let's go
Eh oh eh

There's a bad man coming trying to bring us down
There's a bad man coming trying to bring us down

I got a feeling in my bones
Everything is gonna work out

On a spiritual level
There ain't no mountain
That we can't climb

Hey mister man
Better get yourself a plan

If you think we're gonna fail
Then you're on the wrong track
I can tell by the way that you're choking for breath
You know you're looking at people
Who win

Let's go
We're the people who win

Back on Track

Months turn into years
But I never felt the seasons change
I looked to the sun
I looked to the moon
I called on nature
Mother Nature help me
Help me please

Shouts turned into tears
And it never felt like you were near
I opened my heart
I trusted you and
You said you loved me
Mother Nature help me
Gotta find me a way

And I don't wanna fight
I don't want this to die
Every time I see you near
I wanna tell you that I

I wanna get us back on track
I wanna get us back on track
I wanna get us back on track
I wanna get us back on track
I wanna get us back on track
I wanna get us back on track

Even brave men fear
But you never showed you were aware
You seemed unafraid

We might separate
And I just worry
That we won't get love back
Gotta find me a way

And I don't wanna fight
I don't want this to die
Every time I see you near
I wanna tell you that

I wanna get us back on track
I wanna get us back on track
I wanna get us back on track
I wanna get us back on track

Let the fire of passion burn
We were making love in the morning
Love in the evening
All night

I wanna get us back on track
I wanna get us back on track

I Want That Love

And I'm feeling fine
In my spirit mind
Yeah I'm right there next to you
And you call me baby blue

I won't change my mind
I won't change my mind
And I wonder why I feel the way I do
Well I'll tell you it's you that's who

Everybody tell me that I'm out of my mind
I'll never get you
I'll never get you

Everybody tell me that I'm out of my mind
I'll never get you
I'll never get you

Love
Yeah
Love is all I'm after
Don't care if it last forever
Yeah
Make me feel so fine
Like I'm important
Everybody
Needs somebody

Everybody in this big wide world
Make some time to get some
Every day when the sun goes down

Need that love
Doesn't matter if it's crazy love
I wanna get you on my side
It's not complicated

Everybody
That's everybody
Want some love
It needs no explanation

Everybody
That's everybody
It's love that makes you wanna
Wake up in the morning

Love can bring you pain
It can drive you insane
For all that it's a welcome drug
Feed me on intravenous hugs

Everybody tell me that I'm out of my mind
I'll never get you
I'll never get you

Everybody tell me that I'm out of my mind
I'll never get you
I'll never get you

Love
Yeah
Love is all I'm after
Don't care if it last forever
Yeah
Make me feel so fine
Like I'm important

Everybody
Needs somebody

Everybody in this big wide world
Make some time to get some
Every day when the sun goes down
Need that love
Doesn't matter if it's crazy love
I wanna get you on my side
It's not complicated

Everybody
That's everybody
Want some love
It needs no explanation

Everybody
That's everybody
It's love that makes you wanna
Wake up in the morning

I wanna see you in the noonday sun
Looking bright
I wanna see you in the dead of night
And at the dawning

Everybody
That's everybody
Want some love
It needs no explanation

Everybody
That's everybody
It's love that makes you wanna
Wake up in the morning

Love love love

Yeah I want that love

Everybody
That's everybody
Want some love
It needs no explanation

Everybody
That's everybody
It's love that makes you wanna
Wake up in the morning
Everybody
That's everybody
Want some love
It needs no explanation

Everybody
That's everybody
It's love that makes you wanna
Wake up in the morning

Single Life

People say
They're jealous of me
Asking all the time how I can be so lucky
And how they wish they'd never kissed
The single life goodbye
And why
They struggle every day
To keep from straying

They want my life
They call me a crafty little devil
They think I've got it made
That my streets are paved and golden
And I bathe in sunrays every day

And everybody tell me
Not to be afraid
To gather all the harvest
That the good Lord made

Single life is not what it appears to be
Hope it's not how fate has mapped my life for me
When you sleep
You sleep alone
And you can roll right to the centre of the bed
And you don't have to have strength
For anybody else
And you never have to shout
To defend yourself
You can eat cake and even ice cream
And you can stay out really late

And you can bring home someone
To make you feel special
But it's for a few hours
Then they go away

And everybody tell me
Not to be afraid
To gather all the harvest
That the good Lord made

Single life is not what it appears to be
Hope it's not how fate has mapped my life for me
Single life is not what it appears to be
Hope it's not how fate has mapped my life for me
When I see two people
They look crazy in love
A little bit of heaven
Shining in their eyes
Free and single sounds exciting and it can be
With no warning a great adventure calls
Hitch a ride
Every time I think I've found that someone
I awake

Single life is not what it appears to be
Hope it's not how fate has mapped my life for me
Single life is not what it appears to be
Hope it's not how fate has mapped my life for me
Single life is not what it appears to be
Hope it's not how fate has mapped my life for me

Don't obsess
But I'm looking real hard
It's a spice that I'm missing
From the ingredients

I got freedom
And the money that I work for every day
Could buy me a colour
But it won't buy me a body
I can feel the language
The language of love
That's so universal
Everybody gets to speak it
When they fall in love
That's the end of lonely nights
And
Single life

Starlight

Everyone trying to be somebody
Everybody trying to be someone
Trying to be at the A-list party
But most times on the sidelines waving
Look at me, look at me
Here I am
Here I am, here I am
Can't you see me
Hey

Sell your mother for a breakthrough
And your father if you had to
Living the dream
Chasing the rainbow

Everybody wants to be a starlight
Shining in the darkest hall
Everybody wants to be a starlight
Shining in the darkest hall
Everyone needs something to believe in
Domination is the back-up plan
First thing is to get more notice
Less talk and a lot more action
Look at me, look at me
Here I go
Here I go, here I go
Can't you see me
Hey
Sell your mother for a breakthrough
And your father if you had to

Living the dream
Chasing the rainbow

Everybody wants to be a starlight
Shining in the darkest hall
Everybody wants to be a starlight
Shining in the darkest hall

Even if you see an outside chance
You gotta grab it and big up yourself
A little skinny kid
With shining bright eyes
Yeah

Don't give a reason to get yourself knocked back
You got a personality
Use that
No better place to start than
Right here
Right now
Yeah

Even if you see an outside chance
You gotta grab it and big up yourself
A little skinny kid with shining bright eyes
Yeah

Don't give a reason to get yourself knocked back
You've got a personality
Use that
No better place to start than right here
Right now
Yeah

Always in My Dreams

I visualised your face
I saw the perfect future
Those Freudian dreams
How they captured my desire

I dreamt of you ten times a night
And every image brought you closer
And in my dreams you never left
We made a promise to be together

Now this is real
No counterfeit
You are not my imaginary friend
You are not just a voice inside my head
We've crossed the border
Between truth and dreams

I gave my dream your name
And the story my dream told
Was as vivid and as real
As you standing here
Dreams really do come true
And you're always in my dreams

If I lost you
I'd lose my taste for living
I'd be angry, temperamental and emotional
I'd cry the desperate cry for love
I'd say this was not supposed to happen
But in my dreams we shared a road
We chose to live our life with passion

This might sound strange
But I believe
The heart gives purpose to your life
The head gives way to the heart
Let's live the life
We dared to dream

I gave my dream your name
And the story my dream told
Was as vivid and as real
As you standing here
Dreams really do come true
And you're always in my dreams

Cover My Eyes

I'd like to end up where you've started from
I'd like the happiness you've found
I used to hope you'd look at me like that
But now that hope is fading fast
So I

Cover my eyes
I don't want to see you together
Cover my eyes
Don't be cruel and blind me with your love
How I wish that it was me
Burning up from your sweet kisses
Cover my eyes
'Cause I can't take it

I see you wrapped up in each other's arms
Your synchronising footsteps now
And when you start to fall asleep tonight
You'll spoon and whisper words of love
Please

Cover my eyes
I don't want to see you together
Cover my eyes
Don't be cruel and blind me with your love
How I wish that it was me
Burning up from your sweet kisses
Cover my eyes
'Cause I can't take it

You found your faithful heart

Cover my eyes
Cover my eyes
Cover my eyes
Cover my eyes

How I wish that it was me
Burning up from your sweet kisses
Cover my eyes
'Cause I can't take it

Cover my eyes
I don't want to see you together
Cover my eyes
Don't be cruel and blind me with your love
How I wish that it was me
Burning up from your sweet kisses
Cover my eyes
'Cause I can't take it

I Like It When We're Together

The hours go slowly when you close the door
And you leave me here by myself
How do I fill my days when I feel so sad
Now your warmth has gone away
I bite my lip to stop the tears
But the tears come anyway

I like it when we're together
I don't care if I'm selfish I want you to stay
Everything
Every single thing
Everything I do
I do because I love you

I'm not built to be alone you know
I get anxious when I'm on my own
No need to be opposite sides of doors
No need to talk through walls
I hate that hollow stomach feel
When you turn and walk away

I like it when we're together
I don't care if I'm selfish I want you to stay
Everything
Every single thing
Everything I do
I do because I love you

I like it when we're together
I don't care if I'm selfish I want you to stay
Everything

Every single thing
Everything I do
I do because I love you

I know I make you feel the guilt
And my reasons are emotional
But we can deal with all demons
In their various appearance
Let's remind ourselves how far we've come
Let us look at how we'd really feel
If we turned from each other
Would we ever fall in love again

I like it when we're together
I don't care if I'm selfish I want you to stay
Everything
Every single thing
Everything I do
I do because I love you

I like it when we're together
I don't care if I'm selfish I want you to stay
Everything
Every single thing
Everything I do
I do because I love you

Invisible

The cloak of darkness hides the real you
As you recede into the distance
And you camouflage your feelings
And your wavelength can't be measured

Don't remain invisible to me
'Cause I want you right now
Don't remain invisible to me
'Cause I want you right now

Please let your blue light shine
Let your blue light shine
Let your blue light shine

If I had some magic power
Would I see your reflection
Stumble on some vital signs
To make sense of this perception
Or would you stay invisible
'Cause I want you right now

Don't remain invisible to me
'Cause I want you right now

Please let your blue light shine
Let your blue light shine
Let your blue light shine

Take the bandage from your eyes now
How much better could life be
We are not familiar strangers

But we're not lovers in love
Please don't tease

Don't be invisible to me
'Cause I want you right now
Yeah I want you right now

Please let your blue light shine
Let your blue light shine
Let your blue light shine

Don't let doubts walk all over you
What fears you have you can overcome
Understand what you're running from
Is what you will leave behind

Don't remain invisible to me
'Cause I want you right now
Don't remain invisible to me
'Cause I want you right now

Please let your blue light shine
Let your blue light shine
Let your blue light shine

Loving What You Hate

Sometimes you look in the mirror
Pinpoint every flaw on your face
You say you need so many things to change
Need that beach body
That perfect shape
But as you walk away
I'm loving those things that you hate

I'm loving what you hate
Your brown eyes
I'm loving what you hate
You're too shy
I'm loving what you hate
How you trust everyone
I'm loving you
And I'm loving what you hate

In awkward moments
You grab my hand for support
You hate you looked so innocent
How you laugh when you're embarrassed
You hate the way you talk
Could I love you more
I'm loving those things that you hate

I'm loving what you hate
Your brown eyes
I'm loving what you hate
You're too shy
I'm loving what you hate
How you trust everyone

I'm loving you
Yeah I'm loving what you hate

And as we walk 'round the neighbourhood
You talk to strangers
There is nothing I could hate about you now
Not for a moment
You are just what I'm looking for
Everything about you is what I want
You are just what I'm looking for
Everything about you

Early on
As I got to know you
I noticed little things that I loved about you
The way you smile
How you cherished the simple things
You dance to no music
You love the rain
I'm so in love with you
I love everything about you

I'm loving what you hate
Your brown eyes
I'm loving what you hate
You're too shy
I'm loving what you hate
How you trust everyone
I'm loving you
Yeah and I'm loving what you hate

No More Pain

This pain is my protection
It tells me to run
This pain is what you gave
But it's making me strong
Even though I can't define it
Does not mean that I'm confused

You taught me to grieve
And this hurt is acute
You might be the author of my wounds
But I decide
I decide
I decide
Just how this story will end

This pain
My liberator
This trial
The same
This sting it can treated
Doctor, cure my ills

Misery is my companion
In this sad experience
You stabbed at my heart
And caused it to break
But I know it won't last my whole life long
When I decide
I decide
I decide
That I will stand no more pain

Not Too Far Away

Barbed-wire fencing across the fields
And you're not too far away
Wish you were here instead of there
And not too far away

If I lie in the road
Will you rescue me
If I run through the trees will you see me
Keep me close
In your atmosphere
Life intensifies
When you're near

Put your head on my shoulder
For the rest of your life stay with me
In our cardboard mansion
We will laugh at the rain
And run from the fire straight into the sea
And swim into the unknown you and me

Four in a car, I'm in the back
And you seem so far away
Wish I could drive
I would have you nearer still
And not so far away

If I lie in the road
Will you rescue me
If I run through the trees will you see me
Keep me close
In your atmosphere

Life intensifies
When you're near

Put your head on my shoulder
For the rest of your life stay with me
In our cardboard mansion
We will laugh at the rain
And run from the fire straight into the sea
And swim into the unknown you and me

I want to show you to all my friends
Don't go too far away
The day will come when you'll be mine
And that's not too far away

If I lie in the road
Will you rescue me
If I run through the trees will you see me
Keep me close
In your atmosphere
Life intensifies
When you're near

Put your head on my shoulder
For the rest of your life stay with me
In our cardboard mansion
We will laugh at the rain
And run from the fire straight into the sea
And swim into the unknown you and me

Still Waters

I can picture every detail of your face
As I close my eyes
And in that moment
In that liberating moment
I can wrap you in my arms
Without fear that this will end

But is it really just you and me
How deep still waters run
On the outside we seem ideal
But inside it's not much fun

Like a newborn
I try to hold you
Try to protect you
Scroll through hours
Scroll through days
And scroll through the years
And let's choose the best times
Of this bittersweet love

I can see why we should part and yet still
Inside my head
Is this illusion
Where you run across the room
And lift me up amongst the stars
In your arms
We fly away

But when we fall back to earth we see
How deep still waters run

On the outside we seem ideal
But inside
Inside it's not much fun

Like a newborn
I try to hold you
Try to protect you
Scroll through hours
Scroll through days
And scroll through the years
And let's choose the best times
Of this bittersweet love

Oh it's the silence that hurts more
More than the shouting and the times
When you walk out
Turn back
Turn back
Turn back

Love never moves in straight lines
It bends, it winds
Seeds we've planted
We must cultivate the soil
Not plough the surface of the wounds
With our words that cause the hurt

That's how unattached we are
And how deep still waters run
On the outside we seem ideal
But inside
Inside it's not much fun

Like a newborn
I try to hold you

Try to protect you
Scroll through hours
Scroll through days
And scroll through the years
And let's choose the best times
Of this bittersweet love

This Is Not That

Well this is not that
I'm happy
And I'm jumping over rainbows
Dressed in yellow
Got balloons
And having big fun fun
Do you want some

Tired from trying to be strong
Emotionally drained and looking for a friend
In need of twenty-nine things to make life easy
To make life easy

Well this is not that
I'm happy
And I'm jumping over rainbows
Dressed in yellow
Got balloons
And having big fun fun
Do you want some

The problem with problems
Is that they take up too much time
And too many issues of the heart leave me crying
I'm naked on a mountain but I still don't feel free
You know how frustrating this universe can be

Well this is not that
I'm happy
And I'm jumping over rainbows
Dressed in yellow

Got balloons
And having big fun fun
Do you want some
Do you want some fun

I like beautiful things
You don't buy me diamonds
You don't bring me flowers
I don't wanna feel how much I need you
More than you need me
More than you need me

My head in my hands no signpost at the crossroad
No real solution have we come to a dead end
I'm naked on a mountain but I still don't feel free
You know how frustrating this universe can be
I'm naked on a mountain but I still don't feel free
You know how frustrating this universe can be

Well this is not that
I'm happy
And I'm jumping over rainbows
Dressed in yellow
Got balloons
And having big fun fun
Do you want some
Do you want some fun

Already There

You just told me you loved me
For the very first time
And it feels like I'm flying
And the sky is all mine
I'm floating on air
Let me tell you my secret
I've never said it before
While you were falling in love
I was already there

I was already there
Already there and so in love with you
I was already there

I was already there
But I was biding my time
From that very first touch
I wanted you more than I needed to breathe
The feeling I got
Was more than I knew to expect

The excitement of you was intoxicating
Yeah you took your time to notice me
But I noticed you
And you took my heart
I was already there

I was already there
Already there and so in love with you
I was already there

I was already there
Already there and so in love with you
I was already there

When you came to me crying
From your recent heartache
I would die just a little
But I knew not to fade
In your lonely existence
I could feel your heart change
You were falling in love
But I was already there

I was already there
Already there and so in love with you
I was already there

Do you know you're amazing
Do you know you're amazing

As I bathe in your eyes
Like a ship in the sea
Travelling millions of miles
I float effortlessly into your arms
And in your arms
In your arms
You lifted me

I was already there
Already there and so in love with you
I was already there

I was already there
Already there and so in love with you
I was already there

So in love
I was already there
Already there and so in love with you
I was already there

'Already There' is about love at first sight. I believe when two people fall in love one person is always just ahead of the other. The line that says 'You just told me you love me for the very first time' is when the person finally catches up with the one who fell in love first. Then you have a happy-ending love story.

Better Life

All you want for everyone
Is a better life
A better life

All you want from love
Is the best love
The best love

And all you want from me
Is what I have to give
Just being who you are
Means a better life
A better life

Some people sit in their ivory tower
With the Midas touch
The Midas touch

A kind word has more healing power
It's precious
More precious

Look inside yourself
Make your thoughts the best
All you have to be
Is a love junkie
Love junkie

Change can heal the world
And all you gotta do is change yourself

There are rules for a better life
Don't live with hate
Live positive
Smile a lot
And the world looks good
Your happy face
Looks right back at you

Don't compare yourself
To everybody else
Live the life you love
For a better life
A better life

Change can heal the world
And all you gotta do is change yourself

Memories can last forever
Remember how short a life is
Plan how you will enjoy it
Be happy
Be happy

Look inside yourself
Make your thoughts the best
All you have to be
Is a love junkie
Love junkie

Don't compare yourself
To everybody else
Live the life you love
For a better life
Better life
Better life

Look inside yourself
Make your thoughts the best
Just being who you are
Means a better life
Better life
Better life

Don't compare yourself
To everybody else
Live the life you love
For a better life
Better life
Better life

Consequences

I see your message on the whiteboard
I got your telephone call
When you decide on your choices
Think of the consequences
Think of the consequences

I know you're testing all the boundaries
I see your crocodile tears
I'm gonna keep throwing options
And the consequences
Consequences

I know I know
A little bit me, a little bit you in the blame game
I know I know
Don't wanna lose this beautiful love we've found
And if I can
I'll take away all the pain and the hurt I caused you
I know I know
You wanna do the same
'Cause you want things right again

Finger pointing is aggressive
I'm no angel I know
But don't just follow your impulses
Actions have a voice that cries out
Just tell me what you want me to know

In the end we will be better
If we can sit and talk
No retribution

The past has a part to play in
Decisions we make today
We can't blow the consequences
The consequences

I know I know
It's a little bit me, a little bit you in the blame game
I know I know
We don't wanna lose this beautiful love we've found
And if I can
I'll take away all the pain and the hurt I caused you
I know I know
You wanna do the same
'Cause you want things right again

Don't want a power struggle
I just want to reinforce the trust
And if your actions hurt my heart
I've got to show you just how much
You're testing boundaries
You're pushing limits
Giving in might be easier
To let you win
And bear the consequences

You won't lose your sense of self
Water has a natural way it flows
Let's try hard to work things out
Let's have a plan, A B C and D
Set up guidelines
Keep our cool
Can't maintain the status quo
We got problems
And there are consequences

Don't give me drama and emotion
We're gonna follow this through
We've got to take away restrictions
And face the consequences
I know you're testing all the boundaries
I see your crocodile tears
I'm gonna keep throwing options
And the consequences

I know you're testing all the boundaries
I see your crocodile tears
I'm gonna keep throwing options
And the consequences

I know I know
It's a little bit me, a little bit you in the blame game
I know I know
We don't wanna lose this beautiful love we've found
And if I can
I'll take away all the pain and the hurt I caused you
I know I know
You wanna do the same
'Cause you want things right again

To Anyone Who Will Listen

To anyone who will listen
Please hear what I say
Turn off your judgement
Try and understand
How this lonely heart breaks
How the tears start to fall
I need your help to heal
My troubled mind

To anyone who will listen
To all the possibilities
Just give me the chance
To breathe
To catch my breath
'Cause I'm trying my very best

I'm seeking your comfort
The pressure's released
Just by being here with you
The days are not long
The chance to tell my story
Heals this blue heart
Like medicine you cure
My sleepless nights

To anyone who will listen
To all the possibilities
Just give me the chance
To breathe
To catch my breath
'Cause I'm trying my very best

Be a friend to me
In my despair
Be the friend who never asks why
Even when our conversation is strained
You won't walk out on me
Don't walk out on me

To anyone who will listen
To all the possibilities
Just give me the chance
To breathe
To catch my breath
'Cause I'm trying my very best

To anyone who will listen
Just give me the chance
To breathe
To catch my breath
'Cause I'm trying my very best

This was written after reading an article about a young man who was a
depressive, and all he wanted was for someone to listen to him. Not judge,
not give advice, just listen.

APPENDIX:
HANDWRITTEN LYRICS
AND SCORES

Love and Affection (1976)

Oh the feeling
When your realing
You step lightly thinking your number 1
Down to Zero with a word
I am a
~~for~~ leaving for another one
Now you walk with your feet back
on the ground
Down to the ground Down to the ground
Down to the ground Down to the ground

Brand new dandy first class scene stealer
walks through the crowd and takes your man
Sends you rushing to the mirror
brush your eyebrows and say
There's more beauty in you than anyone
Oh remember who walked the warm sands
beside you
moved to your heels let the waves
come rushing in
She'll take the worries from your head

Down to Zero (1976)

but then again
She'll put trouble in your heart instead
then you'll fall
down to the ground down to the ground

Then you'll know heart ache
Still ~~you~~ more crying
when ~~you~~ thinking of your mothers only
son
Take to your bed
You'll say there's peace in sleep
but you'll dream of love instead
Oh the heart ache you'll find
can bring more pain
than blistering sun
but oh when you fall
oh when you fall
fall at my door
I wanna see a new moon shing through
let me take my love and give it all to you
Oh when you fall

Kissin' and a Huggin' (1977)

Drop the Pilot (1983)

In these times

These are the times
Tears fill the back of your eyes
These are the times
the birds migrate
. across the skies
These are the times
what hope you had you forget
These wicked time
You're bound to feel all sanity is lost

In these times everyone needs love
In these times do you pray to god
In these times everyone needs comfort
And would welcome a hope to hold
your passion is the fire that burns the
hurt that pains the soul
And though my eyes are so polluted
by the sight of lost desires
I still so you can see you standing by

This is my fear
That distance will come between us
And it could mean nothing nothing to get
from here to there
we own the world
And everything that's in it
let our love shine
Like glistening raindrops
resting on a rose

In these times celebrate our love
In these times lets be thankful of
All the days we can spend together

In These Times (2003)

And I'm happy to hold your hand
Your passion is the food that feeds the
hunger in my heart
And now my eyes are clearly open
no more longing for the past
Now I have you in these times

In these everyone needs love
In these times Do you pray to God
In these times everyone needs comfort
and would welcome a hand to hold
Your passion is the fire that burns the
hurt that pains the soul
And though my eyes are so polluted
by the silt of lost desires
Its good to have you in these times.

Once in a while
we share a thought
but most of all we drift apart
haven't you noticed
we seem less happy
more often
And I dont know what to do   C G
whether to be with you   C D
And I sure as sure cant live without you   G   C G
what is to become of us C G
How did we come to this C G
I'm as certain as you   C Am   D   I dont like it
there's something   really   did nothing wrong G C G   (there's something going on)
I've done

When we embrace
the pain is gone
But in reality we hardly touch at all
haven't you noticed
we get more
lonely
more often
And I dont know what to do
whether to be with you
And I'm sure as sure I cant live without you
what is to become of us
Where do we go from here
(I'm as certain as you) I'm as upset as you
~~there's something really wrong~~
At how our love has gone

Less Happy More Often (2003)

Chuck

They're singing secular songs in the
And there's not a word of god
It's all Schubert + Beethoven
Oh and lots of French love songs
So lets go down on Sunday morning
To hear that Jacob sermon read
Everybody dressed in their finest
apparel bags
Listening to the preacher eulogise

Then we'll pray
Yeh we'll pray
our souls rise up upon that day
hallelujah
hallelujah
pray we change to better ways

They're telling stories about love's passion
All about menage a trois
Here those heart felt tender
Coming from that deep bass voice
And whilst some sleep through all this,
Others weep for all the pain   music
As they sing secular songs in the
Churches baby
It's time to kneel lets kneel and pray

Halleluy
Hollm
pray we change to better ways
Then we'll pray
Yey well pray
Our souls will rise upon that day

Secular Songs (2007)

[213]

The sweat of a man
the smell of musk
The noise of the train
from morning till dusk
The up escalator broken down
The clothes on my back
look like they were taken out of
the laundry basket too weary to wash

Now there's hundreds people
pushing and shoving
Sizzling noises coming out of their ears
hold on to the strap
Or hold on to a stranger
hope that stranger's day has not been too hard
Aggression builds up when the going is slow
~~stess~~ and you're packed like sardines
Something's gotta blow.

Something's gotta blow
when you work so hard
And the sweat pours down ~~on you back~~ you
Something's gotta blow   work you slave
When the pay don't match the ~~hours you slave~~
and the pain you get

Something's gotta blow
When ~~you~~ Please stand on the ~~left~~ right
So I can pass on the ~~right~~ left
Cos Something's gotta blow
Something's gonna blow

Something's Gotta Blow (2007)

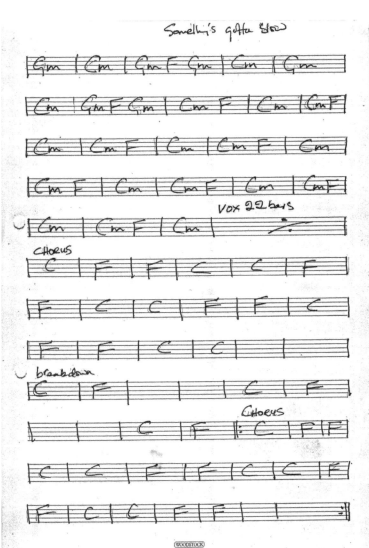

Lyric Credits

Baby I, Back to the Night, Barefoot and Pregnant, Cool Blue Stole My Heart, How Cruel, I Need You, I'm Lucky, Kissin' and a Huggin', Love and Affection, Me Myself I, Opportunity, People, Rosie, Show Some Emotion, The Weakness in Me, Willow, Woncha Come on Home

Already There, Always in My Dreams, All a Woman Needs, Back on Track, Better Life, Blessed, Can't Get Over How I Broke Your Heart, Consequences, Cover My Eyes, Cradled in Your Love, Crazy, Crazy for You, Cry, DNA, Dark Truths, The Devil I Know, Drop the Pilot, Eating the Bear, Empty Highway, Everybody Gotta Know, Everyday Boy, Figure of Speech, Fire and Ice, Free, Frustration, Get in Touch with Jesus, Goddess of Change, He Wants Her, Heading Back to New York City, Help Yourself, I Like It When We're Together, I Love My Baby, I Really Must Be Going, I Want That Love, In These Time, Into the Blues, Invisible, Kind Words and a Real Good Heart, Less Happy More Often, Let's Talk About Us, Liza, Lost the Love, Love Bug, Lovers' Speak, Loving What You Hate, Mama Papa, Merchant of Love, The Messenger, More Than One Kind of Love, No More Pain, Not Too Far Away, Ocean, People Who Win, Physical Pain, Play the Blues, The Power of Dreams, Promise Land, Prove Yourself, Reach Out, Secular Songs, The Shouting Stage, Single Life, Someone's in the Background, Something in the Air Tonight, Something's Gotta Blow, Sometimes I Don't Wanna Go Home, Square the Circle, Starlight, Still Waters, Strange, Talking to the Wall, This Is Not That, Trouble, To Anyone Who Will Listen, A Woman in Love

Index of titles and first lines